Britain in the Past
Anglo-Saxons

Moira Butterfield

Franklin Watts
Published in 2017 by the Watts Publishing Group

Editor: Sarah Ridley
Editor in chief: John C. Miles
Series designer: Jane Hawkins
Art director: Peter Scoulding
Picture research: Diana Morris

Picture credits:
AAA Collection/Alamy: 29. BabelStone/CC Wikimedia: 7b. © The Trustees of the British Museum: 8. www.centingas.co.uk: 25. David Wilson Clarke/dwc-imagery.com: 24. Brian Harris/Alamy: 10b. Jorisvo/Shutterstock: 21. image by Lindsay Kerr : 23. Image by Lindsay Kerr, with thanks to the Wulfheodenas group, www.wulfheodenas.com: 4, 22. Image by Lindsay Kerr, with thanks to Paul Mortimer and the Wulfheodenas group: front cover. Amanda Lewis/Dreamstime: 26. Michelle Middleton Photography: 18. John Miles: 12. Museum of London: 19, 20. G Dali Orti/Art Archive/Alamy: 27. Peter Phipp/Travelshots/Alamy: 28. Image by A.J. Pilkington, with thanks to the Wulfheodenas group: 6, 17. Ann Ronan PL/HIP/Topfoto: 9. scrambled/Dreamstime: 16. David Steele/Shutterstock: 15. CC Wikimedia: 1,13, 14. Colin Young/Dreamstime: 11.

Every attempt has been made to clear copyright. Should there be any inadvertent omission please apply to the publisher for rectification.

Dewey number: 942.01

ISBN: 978 1 4451 4062 9

Printed in China

Franklin Watts
An imprint of
Hachette Children's Group
Part of The Watts Publishing Group
Carmelite House
50 Victoria Embankment
London EC4Y 0DZ

An Hachette UK Company
www.hachette.co.uk

www.franklinwatts.co.uk

Contents

Strangers arrive

Around 1,600 years ago a great change happened in England and Wales. The Romans had ruled for 400 years, but in 410 CE the Roman army left. People living at that time faced an uncertain future.

▲ Re-enactors pose as invading warriors.

Look!

Many of the new settlers came to Britain because they wanted good land to farm. The areas they came from often flooded, so they were not good for growing crops. In southern Britain there was better soil and less flooding.

Land-snatching settlers

Tribes began to raid southern Britain from all around, stealing what they could. Then people from the areas we now call Germany and Denmark began to arrive and take over land.

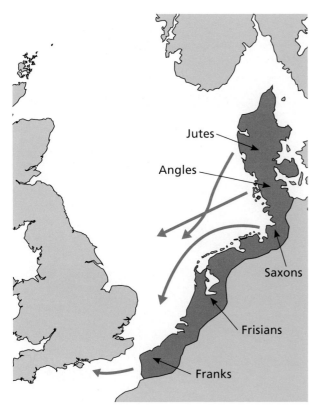

▲ This map shows who invaded Britain in the 400s-500s CE and where they came from.

We call these settlers the Anglo-Saxons. Some of the new arrivals were warriors who fought for power. Others were farming families who set up their own villages.

All change

What exactly happened during this time is unclear but we do know that there was some fighting between local Britons and the invaders. Around 500 CE there was a big battle at Badon Hill, probably somewhere near Bath or Bristol, and the Britons pushed back the invaders for a while. But in the end the invaders controlled southern Britain and many Britons were forced to flee.

A new kind of life

The new settlers lived very differently to the Romans who had ruled Britain before them. They built thatched wooden huts, not grand stone buildings, and they believed in different gods and goddesses. All of the people who were living in England at this time came to be called the Anglo-Saxons.

Meet some warriors

The Anglo-Saxons were ruled by warlords who split the country into different kingdoms. These local kings sometimes fought each other for land and power.

Live like a warrior

Each warlord had a band of loyal warriors called thanes who swore to fight for him to the death. If you were a warrior you lived with your leader in his wooden hall and spent your days training for battle.

These re-enactors carry replica Anglo-Saxon weapons. ▼

Fighting style

Anglo-Saxon warriors rode to battle on horseback but they fought on foot with spears, knives, axes or swords. They wore iron helmets and chainmail shirts, and they carried wooden shields. In battle, groups of warriors lined up in front of each other, overlapping their shields to make a 'shieldwall'. They shouted, threw spears and then charged, trying to break through their enemy's shieldwall.

Dead mens' weapons

We know something about weapons and shields of the time because early Anglo-Saxon warriors were buried with them. Early Anglo-Saxons were pagan, which means they believed in many gods and goddesses. They believed that when people died they went, not to Heaven, but to an afterlife where they needed their possessions (see p10). Warriors were buried with weapons and occasionally even a horse to use in the afterlife.

Look!

The triangular-shaped Anglo-Saxon knife blade shown above is called a seax. It was found in the River Thames and it is now in the British Museum. It has its owner's name – Beagnoth – written on it along with an alphabet of runes (letter symbols of the time). It's possible the runes were put on as a magical spell to help give the knife power.

Join in a feast

Anglo-Saxon warlords based themselves in wooden halls along with their warriors, who were treated to feasting, music and storytelling.

Inside a hall

An Anglo-Saxon hall was dark and shadowy inside. It was lit by a smoky roaring fire in the hearth and candles made from rushes dipped in animal fat. The walls were hung with animal skins and tapestries to keep the cold out, and the wooden pillars and roof might have been carved and painted. The leader probably had a wooden throne while his followers sat on benches.

Feasting fun

At feasting time the warriors ate the roasted meat of animals they had hunted. They drank beer or a strong alcoholic drink called mead, made from honey.

Look!

This drinking horn was buried with a wealthy Anglo-Saxon leader in Taplow, Buckinghamshire. It is made from the horn of a giant cow called an auroch and it was used at feasts and ceremonies. The leader was buried with his drinking horn so he could feast in the afterlife.

The Taplow drinking horn, from the 500s. ▼

As they ate, harpists and lyre-players played music.

Storytelling time

Storytelling was very popular in Anglo-Saxon times. After a feast a storyteller told a traditional

If you were an Anglo-Saxon...

Anglo-Saxons loved riddles, and during a feast you might hear some. Everybody would try to guess what object the riddle was about. Here is one to try:

When I am alive I do not speak.
Anyone can take me captive and cut off my head.
I do no harm to anyone unless they cut me first.
Then I make them cry!

Answer: An onion

tale of heroes, battles and magical monsters. The stories that we know of were about bravery in battle, loyalty and courage in the face of death. The warriors listening in the hall

▲ A scene from the Bayeux Tapestry (see p29) showing an Anglo-Saxon king feasting.

would have greatly admired the fearless story heroes.

Bury a pagan

Early Anglo-Saxons did not write things down, but we can tell something about what they believed from the things that have been found in their graves.

Taking it with you

Pagan Anglo-Saxons thought that the dead lived in an afterlife similar to life on Earth. Warriors needed weapons, kings needed treasure and ordinary people needed everyday objects such as knives or pots.

A king in a boat

One of the greatest Anglo-Saxon treasure hoards ever found came from a local Anglo-Saxon king's grave in Sutton Hoo, Suffolk. When the king died he was buried inside a wooden boat, perhaps to take him on

If you were an Anglo-Saxon...

If you had been at Sutton Hoo when the king was buried, you could have watched his faithful warriors honour their fallen leader. They laid the dead king inside a burial chamber on the ship, surrounded by his treasures, as shown in this museum exhibit.

a journey to the afterlife. He even had a gold and jewel-decorated purse full of money to pay the ghostly oarsmen thought to row him on his trip. His burial boat was placed under a big mound of earth.

Look!

Many historians believe the person buried at Sutton Hoo is Raedwald, king of the East Angles. He converted to Christianity around 600 CE, and some Christian objects were found in the grave at Sutton Hoo. But in life he also kept pagan traditions as well.

Packed for the afterlife

The Sutton Hoo king was buried along with costly well-crafted fighting equipment, including a helmet, sword and shield. He had piles of clothes to ensure he looked smart, including linen shirts, cloaks and furry caps. He even had the things he needed for feasting, such as a drinking horn, silver bowls and spoons.

A reconstruction of the helmet discovered at Sutton Hoo. ▶

Visit a monastery

In 597 monks arrived in southern Britain from Christian Europe. They began to convert the pagan Anglo-Saxons to Christianity, and soon Anglo-Saxons became monks and nuns themselves.

▲ St Laurence's Church in Wiltshire dates from the 700s.

Living in a monastery

Large monasteries (called abbeys) and small ones (called priories) were soon dotted around the country. Monks lived there and spent their days praying or working. Monasteries had gardens, farms and kitchens, so there was lots to do. The monks and nuns wore long robes called habits, with a belt tied round the middle. Monks and nuns still wear similar clothes today, over a thousand years later!

Look!

The earliest Anglo-Saxon churches were small simple-looking buildings made of wood or stone, where ordinary people went to hear their local priest tell them about the Bible. Some of these churches still exist today.

A promise to God

People who joined a monastery had to live by strict rules that governed what they did every hour of the day. They prayed together every few hours, from early morning to late evening. They made promises to obey their church leaders, to give up all their possessions and never to marry or have children.

The first English authors

Unlike ordinary people, Anglo-Saxon monks were taught to read and write. They wrote the first English history books we know of, and the first English poems, too. The most famous monk-author was Bede, who lived in the 700s in a monastery near Jarrow in Tyne and Wear. He wrote a history of the English, describing some of the things that happened in Anglo-Saxon times.

If you were an Anglo-Saxon...

Ordinary Anglo-Saxon children did not go to school, but if you were a bright child you might be sent to a monastery or nunnery from the age of seven, to learn to be a monk or a nun. Bede (shown above) was sent to a monastery when he was seven, and he spent the rest of his life there.

Paint with gold

Anglo-Saxon monks illustrated their writing with tiny pictures and patterns, called illumination. The books they made were rare and valuable treasures, used in churches or by wealthy people.

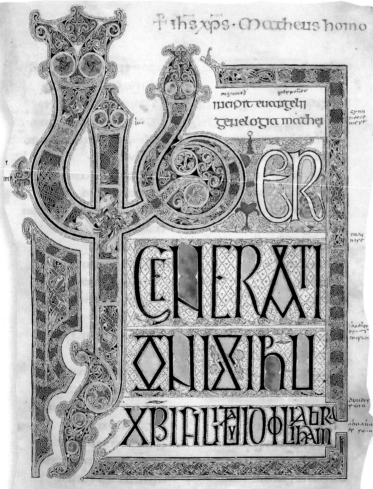

▲ A page from the *Lindisfarne Gospels*. The swirling patterns were a popular art style at the time.

Illuminating inks

Monks wrote and painted in a room called a scriptorium. They used pens cut from bird feathers or reeds and dipped them in an inkwell made from animal horn. The coloured inks were made from ground-up plants, rocks and animals.

Top treasure

The most famous surviving Anglo-Saxon book is the *Lindisfarne Gospels*, created some time in the early 700s at Lindisfarne Priory in Northumberland. The book was probably the work of one man, possibly a monk called Eadfrith.

Parchment, not paper

Nobody in England knew how to make paper in Anglo-Saxon times. Instead monks wrote on parchment made from animal skin. The monks made it themselves, soaking, scraping, cleaning and stretching it. Once the pages were written and painted, the monks sewed them together to make a book, which was covered in leather and sometimes decorated with expensive jewels.

Holy Island, where the *Lindisfarne Gospels* were created, is still cut off from the mainland twice a day. ▼

If you were an Anglo-Saxon...

If you were a monk in a scriptorium you would have written in Latin but, like other Anglo-Saxons, have spoken Old English, which sounded very different from English today. Here's an Old English sentence, and a modern translation:

Wod pa wiges heard, weapon up ahof.
A war-like Viking came forward, weapon raised.

Look!

In 793 Lindisfarne Priory was attacked by Vikings (see p18). Some monks were killed but others escaped, taking the *Lindisfarne Gospels* with them. It was very lucky that the book survived.

Visit a village

Ordinary Anglo-Saxon people lived in villages and farmed small strips of land to feed their families. Farming peasants were called ceorls (pronounced 'churls').

Inside a house

A ceorl's house looked rather like a large modern shed. It was wooden with no windows and it had a thatched roof but no chimney. Indoors, it must have been a smoky place to live as a fire was always burning. There might have been a couple of rooms, with just a few wooden pieces of furniture on the earth floor.

This reconstructed ceorl's house is at West Stow Anglo-Saxon Village in Suffolk. ▼

Look!

Anglo-Saxon homes did not have toilets or running water. The toilet was a hole in the ground outside, and people washed using water from streams. You can see a reconstructed Anglo-Saxon village at West Stow in Suffolk. Don't worry – you won't have to use a hole for a toilet!

Working to survive

Families spent their days looking after their crops and farm animals. They had to grow enough to feed themselves, and if their crops failed they faced starvation. As well as the food they grew, they gathered edible wild plants, fruit and nuts from the woods around their village. They had to be practical people, able to make their own tools and clothes.

◀ Anglo-Saxons had to be practical, making everything they needed using just a few tools.

Called to fight

Ceorls only owned land because their local king allowed them to. In return they promised to fight for him when he needed them. The men in a village could be called up to fight in a local army, called a *fyrd*. When they got the call they had to travel away from home, carrying whatever weapons they owned, to meet up with the fyrd and get ready for battle.

If you were an Anglo-Saxon...

Even if you were a lowly farmer, you might own a slave to help you with your work. Slavery was common at this time. Slaves were either people captured in battle, born as slaves or forced into slavery because they could not pay a debt.

Beat back the Vikings

At the end of the 700s Viking raiders sailed across from Scandinavia to Britain. At first they raided the coast, stealing church treasures and local people to sell as slaves. Then they began to stay, killing Anglo-Saxon leaders and taking land for themselves.

Wessex heroes

The Vikings conquered parts of the south, east and north of England. Only one Anglo-Saxon leader, King Alfred of Wessex, was left standing in their way. He was very nearly defeated but he rallied the men in his kingdom and won a great victory over the Vikings at the Battle of Edington in 878. After this defeat the Vikings agreed to rule their own part of England, called the Danelaw, and leave Alfred to rule Wessex.

This Viking re-enactor wears a helmet and chainmail shirt and carries a sharp sword and wooden shield.▶

Look!

You can see Viking spears and axes at the Museum of London, evidence of the fighting that went on between the Anglo-Saxons and their Scandinavian enemies. The weapons were found in the River Thames where they may have been thrown after a battle.

▲ A Viking battleaxe head.

Facing the Vikings

It would have been terrifying to face an attack from Viking warriors. They arrived on the coast in long narrow warships. They were prepared to fight to the death because they believed that dying in battle would allow them into *Valhalla*, a heavenly feasting hall for dead heroes. One Anglo-Saxon writer compared them to stinging hornets or ferocious wolves.

Winning back the kingdom

Over time Alfred's son, daughter and grandson gradually pushed back the Vikings, fighting to win back the land the invaders had taken. But the Vikings didn't go away – they settled in the Danelaw and eventually integrated with the locals.

If you were Anglo-Saxon...

If you were an Anglo-Saxon caught by the Vikings, you might have been taken off to be sold in a slave market in Ireland, North Africa or Eastern Europe. You might never have seen your family and friends again.

Go to town

Over time Anglo-Saxons began to live in towns, setting up markets and workshops there.

Look!

The Anglo-Saxons made their own coins. The penny coin below was found in London (called *Lundenwic* or *Lundenburg* in Anglo-Saxon times). It is made of silver and shows the head of King Alfred.

Muddy living

Anglo-Saxon towns were very small compared to today's towns. The thatched wooden homes of the townsfolk were built along a few muddy tracks and the only stone building might have been a church. Craftsmen such as blacksmiths, potters and weavers set up their workshops in towns because there were plenty of customers there. There would be market stalls, too, selling local food.

New walls, new names

King Alfred of Wessex had walls and ditches built around the towns of Wessex to keep out the Vikings. He called these defended towns *burhs*. Villagers from the nearby countryside could flee inside the walls if there

◀ The silver coin includes the words 'ALFRED REX' meaning King Alfred.

was any danger of an attack. Many Anglo-Saxon towns still survive as modern towns. Do you recognise any of these Anglo-Saxon place-name endings, still used today?

-bury, -ford, -ham, -ton, -wick

▲ The Anglo-Saxons built a cathedral at Winchester. Later it was rebuilt using the old cathedral stones and this is the building you can see today.

Alfred's capital

Alfred made Winchester the capital of his kingdom. Here he had his palace and held court with his advisors. He was the first English ruler to have the laws of the land properly written down and he founded some of the first schools. He was buried in the abbey at Winchester, though his bones were later moved and were lost. Archaeologists are still trying to work out what happened and perhaps even find his remains.

If you were an Anglo-Saxon...

Travelling wasn't easy. If you wanted to get to a town from your village you would have to trudge along muddy forest tracks, braving wild animals such as boars and wolves and risking attack from lawless bandits.

Get dressed

We can tell what Anglo-Saxons wore by looking at pictures from the time and studying ancient objects such as the jewellery.

Everyday clothes

Ordinary men wore linen shirts and woolly tunics over the top, with a belt and woolly trousers or leggings. Ordinary women wore long linen dresses with a long woolly pinafore tunic and a belt on top.

Re-enactors wear modern copies of Anglo-Saxon clothes. ▼

If you were an Anglo-Saxon...

In Anglo-Saxon times you wouldn't have worn underpants. It's possible that you might have worn a linen loin cloth wrapped around you like a nappy, but nobody knows for sure. You might have worn woollen socks to keep your feet warm in winter.

This Anglo-Saxon necklace contains beads made from amber and amethyst. ▶

Women spent a lot of their time spinning thread from sheep's wool and weaving it into cloth, using a loom set up in their home. Anglo-Saxon children dressed like their parents.

Top fashion

Wealthy nobles and churchmen wore fine embroidered clothing made from expensive cloth. Their jewellery was made by skilled craftspeople using gold and precious stones. We know that Anglo-Saxon fashions changed over time, and wealthy people would probably have kept up with the new styles.

A hairy time in history

Anglo-Saxon women wore their hair long. They pinned it under a veil that covered their head and shoulders. We know that men were very proud of their long hair and beards. Anyone who cut off a man's beard against his will could be fined 20 shillings! Monks and slaves were probably the only people who had their hair cut short.

Look!

Anglo-Saxons loved jewellery, especially rings, brooches and bead necklaces. Both men and women pinned brooches on their clothes to fasten them (buttons hadn't been invented yet).

Celebrate!

The Anglo-Saxons celebrated festivals and special family events such as weddings, just as we do today.

A promise and a party

When Anglo-Saxons got married they made a promise called a *wedd*, from which we get the name 'wedding'. We don't know what the ceremony was exactly, but we know that there would have been a feast, with special cakes and toasts drunk to the bride and groom. The happy couple wore their best clothes and the bride wore flowers in her hair. It sounds familiar, doesn't it? Some of our modern wedding traditions come from this time.

◄ This Anglo-Saxon stone carving shows a 'wedd' between a man and a woman.

Look!

Pagan Anglo-Saxons celebrated a spring festival dedicated to their goddess Eostre. They wore flowers, danced and feasted. When Christianity took over, the festival became Easter.

Christmas

Before Anglo-Saxons became Christian they celebrated the beginning of the year, around 25 December, by holding a feast on *Modraniht* (Mother's Night). They decorated their homes with evergreen tree

branches and burned a huge log in the fireplace. When Christianity came to Britain, some of these celebrations were adapted for Christmas. We hold a feast and bring trees into our homes.

Games and fun

When Anglo-Saxon people gathered together to celebrate festivals, they liked to play sport. They joined in tug-of-war competitions, swimming races and wrestling matches. They also played games with wooden

▲ Re-enactors celebrate Christmas in an Anglo-Saxon hall filled with candles, food and evergreen branches.

If you were an Anglo-Saxon...

If you were a pagan Anglo-Saxon your year would have been marked by regular sacrifices to your gods to keep them happy and ensure you had a good harvest. At festival times you might offer them special cakes or cooked meat.

sticks and balls, a little like hockey and baseball.

Visit an abbey

Abbeys were very important places in Christian Anglo-Saxon times. They held sacred holy treasures that were thought to be magical.

Holy healers

Britain's most important abbeys held relics, the remains of saints. Saints' body parts were buried in decorated tombs. People made journeys called pilgrimages to visit these holy places, where the saints were thought to grant miracles such as healing the sick.

A place of pilgrimage

One of the most important late Anglo-Saxon shrines was at Bury St Edmunds in Suffolk. Here lay the bones of King Edmund, a Christian king killed by the pagan Vikings in 869. The Vikings tied Edmund to a tree and shot him with arrows.

The abbey ruins at Bury St Edmunds in Suffolk. ▼

Top trouble

Abbeys were run by bishops and archbishops – top-ranking churchmen who crowned kings and advised them. For instance, in 1066 an archbishop called Stigand crowned King Harold at Westminster Abbey. He is pictured on the Bayeux Tapestry, which tells the tale of what happened in 1066. Two other people thought they should be king, and when Stigand put the crown on Harold's head he helped to bring about disaster for the Anglo-Saxons (see p28)!

(see p28)

If you were an Anglo-Saxon...

A pilgrimage could take weeks, but you would think it was worth it because visiting a holy site would help get you into Heaven. If you were very wealthy you might make a pilgrimage to Rome, the home of the Pope who was the leader of the Christian Church at that time.

This panel from the Bayeux Tapesty shows King Harold (middle, with the crown on his head) and Archbishop Stigand to the right. ▼

A deadly battle

King Harold was crowned in January 1066, but in October he lost the kingdom and his life when Anglo-Saxon rule came to an end on the battlefield at Hastings.

▲ The Battle of Hastings re-enacted, with the Normans on horseback.

Two enemies

Harald Hardrada, King of Norway, claimed the kingdom from Harold. So too did William, Duke of Normandy in France. In the autumn of 1066 Harold had to march his army north to defeat Hardrada at Stamford Bridge in Yorkshire. Just a few days later William invaded from the south and Harold had to rush his forces back to defend his kingdom.

If you were an Anglo-Saxon...

William's victory led to a confusing time for local people. The new rulers spoke a different language and instead of wooden halls they based themselves in stone castles which they built around the kingdom. Anglo-Saxons had to get used to tough new laws or face punishment.

A new ruler

Harold's men met William's invading army near Hastings in Sussex. The battle was long and hard, but eventually King Harold was killed, his army was defeated and Duke William marched up to London to be crowned in Westminster Abbey. King William shared out the conquered land between his French followers.

This scene from the Bayeux Tapestry may show the moment when Harold was killed (below, left). ▼

All change

Anglo-Saxon nobles lost their land and power. Some were killed in battle and others fled abroad. Meanwhile ordinary people found they had new French-speaking rulers. William changed the laws, taking away rights and imposing higher taxes.

Look!

Soon after William's invasion the story was embroidered, probably by Anglo-Saxon women, on a giant roll of linen called the Bayeux Tapestry. The tapestry is on display in Bayeux, France, and there is a copy at the Museum of Reading in Berkshire.

Glossary

Afterlife The idea that the dead live on in a different world.

Burh An Anglo-Saxon town with a defensive wall and ditch around it.

Ceorl An Anglo-Saxon peasant.

Christian Someone who believes that Jesus Christ is the son of God.

Drinking horn A hollow curved decorated animal horn for drinking liquid.

Fyrd A group of ordinary men called up from villages to fight for their local leader.

Habit A robe worn by a monk or a nun.

Hearth troop An Anglo-Saxon leader's closest, most trusted warriors.

Illumination A beautiful decoration painted around writing.

Mead An alcoholic drink made from honey.

Monastery A place where monks live and pray.

Normans Nobles from Normandy in France.

Old English The language spoken by Anglo-Saxons.

Pagan Someone who believes in many gods and goddesses.

Parchment A document made from animal skin.

Pilgrimage A journey made to a holy place.

Relic A holy object thought to have magical powers.

Runic alphabet Writing symbols used by the Anglo-Saxons.

Saint A dead religious hero or heroine thought to have the power to send miracles.

Scriptorium A room in a monastery where monks wrote and decorated documents.

Seax A triangular-shaped knife blade.

Shieldwall A row of warriors with their shields interlocked.

Thane An important and wealthy Anglo-Saxon.

Viking Someone from the kingdoms of Scandinavia.

Further information

Weblinks

http://www.museumoflondonimages.com
Go to the Anglo-Saxon section to see objects found around London.

http://anglosaxondiscovery.ashmolean.org/index.html
Meet the Anglo-Saxons and play games and activities.

http://www.bbc.co.uk/history/british/normans/launch_gms_battle_hastings.shtml
Play the Battle of Hastings Game to re-enact the battle.

http://www.bayeuxtapestry.org.uk
See the Bayeux Tapestry online.

Note to parents and teachers: Every effort has been made by the Publishers to ensure that the web sites in this book are suitable for children, that they are of the highest educational value, and that they contain no inappropriate or offensive material. However, because of the nature of the Internet, it is impossible to guarantee that the contents of these sites will not be altered. We strongly advise that Internet access is supervised by a responsible adult.

Timeline

410 CE The Roman army left Britain to the mercy of invaders.

556 CE There were seven kingdoms in southern Britain.

597 CE Augustine arrived to convert people to Christianity.

625 CE approx An important leader was buried at Sutton Hoo.

672 CE Bede, the chronicler of Anglo-Saxon history, was born.

793 CE The Vikings attacked Lindisfarne Abbey.

878 CE Alfred, King of Wessex, defeated a Viking army at the Battle of Edington.

937 CE King Athelstan became king of all Britain after defeating the Scots and Vikings at the Battle of Brunanburg.

1016 CE Danish Viking Canute ruled Britain.

1042 CE Anglo-Saxon kings returned with the crowning of Edward the Confessor.

1066 CE The Battle of Hastings ended Anglo-Saxon rule forever.

Index